Awesome You

YUSIMI

To order additional copies of this book, contact:
Xlibris
844-714-8691
www.Xlibris.com
Orders@Xlibris.com

ISBN: Softcover   978-1-6698-4838-7
            EBook   978-1-6698-4839-4

Print information available on the last page

Rev. date: 09/27/2022

Dedication

I dedicated this book to my kids Ethan and Liam

Angels of Love

Angels they are
Angels of love
Angels the children,
A true feeling of love.

Peace and caring,
You finally have
A gift of the God,
Children of love.

Wisdom to children
You give with love,
Loving the children,
Never left, home.

Our life are our children,
They are our true home,
Angels of love.

The Chocolate Lover

Chocolate, chocolate
lover of chocolate,
Chocolate milk,
Chocolate cookie,
And ice cream.
You my boy, love chocolate
So much!
So much!
My chocolate boy,
You
Always be,
My son!
My love!
You always be,
My chocolate lover,
Your wish is so easy to give.
You give me a smile,
I will make your dream
You will see,
The chocolate lover
My love you always be,
Let's go together, for a chocolate milk with marshmallows and cream.

It is a dream

Silence the night and everyone sleeping,
Silence come to me,
I am thinking,
Thinking of you,
Thinking of the Mountain,
Rivers and sea.
Night is silence,
I want your silence to be,
Parts of me.
I ask for adventure,
But the Universe is silent,
I want to learn,
A wish this dream,
to come,
to me....
It is a dream,
I will, will be,
A dream to come to me,
It is night and I will go to sleep.
I will follow my dreams.

Treasures of life

The day go,
the day pass,
And I have,
the treasures of life,
My friends, my companions,
Day and night.

When family is away,
I have my friends,
The treasure of life
Like air
Like water.
They know you better,
like mother know her children,
Your friends are the soul
Must beautifully gift.
of love and respect,
the teach.
And is a friend,
The treasures of life, it is,
like brothers and sisters
our friends.

Unique is your love

You know, my love,
You are one love,
A unique soul of love.
Full like the moon,
I have all you,
For me,
My awesome you.
You are,
Unique as you are,
My love, my love.
I give and I love to give this to you,
With love
Yes, I do!
My time,
My love.
"I love you,"
You are, unique my love,
Remember that,
Take care of You,
And always be good,
And do good, be you,
Believe in you.

Flow like water

Like water is fresh,
Your heart must be clean,
Your beautiful feeling,
A kiss and a smile,
Full of dream.

Fresh water that flow,
and
Drops of love,
Full of peace,
Be
Persisted,
Keep going
And dream.
Believe in your dream
To be
Like water flow,
Protect,
Your dreams to be.

Blue sky

When you look up and see the blue sky,
Searching for feeling to go away,
And a white cloud pass by,
The feeling is so good,
I smile.
The beauty of nature,
The magic of the blue sky.

Take away your emotion,
And relax your feeling.
Is the blue-sky magic?
is beauty
I spoke,
Nothing is impossible
You see
To make you see the beauty,
you accept
And be happy.
Go and follow
Your dream.
The blue-sky whispers.

Big and strong like a tree

My little seed,
Green little tree,
You are young but know,
Were you are going with your dream,
Are you want to be strong like a tree,
With green, yellow, red leaf.
Yes! you will
And you are strong,
You are,
And you will survive,
The winter,
The summer,
The spring,
The fall,
So be
Strong like a tree,
Big and strong beautiful tree.
I love each little leaf and flower you give.

Little child keeps smiling

Little child keeps going and be,
The smile of my life.

Little boy you are loved,
Be the good man
a girl dreams.

Smile to me and keep motivating me,
And keep trying
And be happy
And little man keeps smiling
For me,
For everyone.
You are the most beautiful boy
That had shown to me happiness.

You

You
Where are you going,
My boy remembers
I will be here for you.
My boy,
My son,
My love and life.
Tell me your dreams
be what you will do
For you
I want to be here and help you,
You will see
Be you,
Be patience and you will be.

Start with you

It is another day for you and me
To start and work on your dreams,
For your kids
That you love,
For those little things, that you will be,
Be strong and keep going and be you.
Awesome start you are,
and accomplish what you need
keep going
give all,
your effort,
and attention,
And trying
And you will have,
the knowledge
The wisdom
You love to see
Is you
your true.

Happy

Happy moments
And spaces,
That you know that make you happy,
Is true and hold them
GO
And be happy.
Be that part that make me
Happy, that part that is you,
And I love on you.

Good and reality,
Perfection and great,
Adoration and good,
Good will.
Play well
And believe,
As happy as you can be.
Be happy always to be
The happy boy you want to be.

Happy is the way you made me feel when you kiss me
The way I feel when I see you
And the time we spend together.
Is one love you will never left

Love

Love is born and stay with you,
But the time will come, and you must protect
Your love to stay always with you.
Love with you always be,
A kiss,
A hug and smile,
Always stay with you.
Love stays with him,
My sweet love my precious child,

I love you
I love you
Love stays with him
And you
Teach your love to every child.

Daylight of happiness

In my arms you are,
and I feel your Golding heart,
that,
I have my child,
with an imagination full of adventures,
Daylight of happiness,
Light of joy,
In my arms this light,
I found, is love,
Delightful my joy,
Full of passion.
With Golding heart, I feel the passion, that make you strong,
to be courageous,
Daylight of happiness,
Full of glad and deep affection,
Warm is your heart, you are my passion,
My daylights of happiness, Days by days,
You give me light,
You are delightful.

Small Kisses

I am so lucky today,
You give me a kiss,
But your kisses are specials,
Those small kisses you give,
kisses with trust,
That give me so much,

Love and my confidence,
I feel stronger,
You kiss me like this,
you give me a kiss,
A small kiss with love,
Of love,
Small kisses that said,
I promise,
and I will,
True love you are,
Small kisses that make you believe.

We can do it

I know where we are going
My love my baby
Mountains are tall
Trees are green
And we can do it baby
We will get there.

We will be fine
And you keep going
Through the sea
Over the rocks
And dark nights
We will go and go.

We can do it baby
Listen to yourself
You can move mountain
You will be ok and safe,
You can do it baby
Keep going you are strong.

Don t let go

Don let go your hands and stay near me
Be my inspiration to keep going
and let my heart heir your voice.

Let's walk together and pick up the flowers
Let's adore their color and perfume
Walking together like mother and child
Expressing our love.

I love that is forever
I love that will never go.
Love your parents without stopping
be good kids
Full of respect and love
Full of devotion.

Let hug strong
And see the beautiful start
Day and night
I will love you like this
My lovely child nothing can break our love.
Is all for you and is beautiful

You are my dream

When I woke up is for you
I walk and decide to move on
for you

I think on you all the time
And your smile is my treasure
Thank you!
For making my dreams come true.

I will tell you that my love for you is infinity
And the true is that is beautiful
And is all for you darling
your love is what make me happy.

I found my owns devotion and adorer you
Is something beautiful baby
So, stay kind my love,
You are beautiful
Yes! you are a shine start on the sky.

Together

I enjoy our moment
That pass so fast,
The beauty delirium to see your smiling.

Each day you are growing so fast and is good
I will miss this time togethers, you and me
I will keep your memories on my heart,
And your
expression on front of me,
That only can Touch my soul.

That keep my life strong for you
To be better and dream

Stay stronger
To enjoy your days
And each day be happy
You know well what love it is.
Togethers like this, I kiss your forehead
And send you my blessing
For you, from me with love and care.
You are my number one and only

You and I

And I feel this way
Smiling and thinking of you
I wonder all the think I want to say
And I finally found love when you are
When I hug you or I kiss you
I am happy for that
love

I am glad you are mind
And I smile
I am in love
I think
Finally, I feel metamorphosis
You all what I want
I am happy to see you smiling
And this love is all I need
You are my only the one my number one
and only I love you

My last love you are
You are better than gold
Time fly
And you baby
You are better than gold
The time we are together
is better than gold
When you come to me and ask
I will respond
with respect
I feel proud of your accomplishments
I love how you are
You are strong and I could be more proud
To love you each day
To be by your side
And together keep going and never stop
Because you are better than gold.

Teach me I want to learn

I want to learn
About the moon
And the night
The start and the sky
I want to be your best student
The only one
I hope you teach me right
I already have taught you
so much
Let me learn from you
now
The time is short,
and life pass fast
Let's learn together to be
better
To be
good and kind
To respect
To love
To give.

You will be on my heart
I remember
First time I saw you
I was so happy to be with you
I want it to time stop
and expend my life with you
I saw you
my moment and life change
For a moment
I smile and I did say
I know how to love I will love you all my life
You will be on my heart baby
Everywhere I go
I will think of you
I will love you forever and you
Will be always with me in my heart
You are my everything
Believe on me
I believe on you.

Printed in the United States
by Baker & Taylor Publisher Services